I0764686

No Matter

by Jennifer Burch

A product of the Winged Way

This book is an offering of the Winged Way, an organization dedicated to the generation, presentation, and distribution of value. For more information visit www.wingedway.com.
FIRST EDITION
ISBN 978-0-6152-0223-5

Thanks to the following publications for including some of these works in earlier forms: Article Journal, Free Verse, Guernica, Sal Mimeo, and Verse.

[Last Night]

I saw a shadow on the wall,
but did not know the figure there.
A fierce hand reached out.
It settled in my bed.
I wished it were not mine.

In a room of frames,
her shirt falls down.
The chair, the floor, the frames,
and the room–
none of them are true.
Another breast pushes through.
He repeats her. Repeats a sky.
It comes in sleep.
Some eyes are finished.

You enter and are born. Matter meant to be transformed. *Be still, fly, die.* The will to move is separate, assumes edges, cannot decide. This is bondage, a costume followed by desire. Nature perpetuates delusion, then returns. She relives and she relieves illusion.

The fishes are a figment of our holding.
In death this blue will inundate,
and light strike sea with human wishes.
The fishes are a figment of our holding.
The child raped by world has given birth
to flood. Her voices held in shells,
her body in the swells of water mountains.

The water grew more distant from the cliff the longer you looked, so you jumped. The wild things under the bed, trapped behind one-way closet doors in the night, disappeared into the brightness of adolescence, or under blue skies in the suburbs.

If that's the stuff little boys are made of, then:
I'll stick my lips to the flat reflection of the world,
my tongue to the cold flag pole.
Along will come a little boy
who flicks a match to warm the world
and frees my lips and tongue to taste
and say: it's a freedom to have a tongue, girl,
chopsticks to contact or spork to mouth.

In a fishnet, he impressed a young version. But today he woke up as Katherine Hepburn, played tennis, and trembled around the house. He was alone in a fancy voice.

When they say blow or breathe
into, think of crops and a
swollen cheek, disease unseen in
linens—one protrusion could
replace a wound.

In a fishnet, he impressed a young version. But today he woke up as Katherine Hepburn, played tennis, and trembled around the house. He was alone in a fancy voice.

When they say blow or breathe into, think of crops and a swollen cheek, disease unseen in linens—one protrusion could replace a wound.

Space separates where lines join,
not a word, not a tender.
I imagine it will go no further,
the bodies, surfaces forced apart in frames
extend severally, individually.

Thought was moving one way, the other not. Think not returning. All hush around. What riddles are they telling? He said "say". Imagine two lovers, one on land, the other in air he speaks to. If this could be criteria, as though there's something to meet. How space slows down. After years in chairs. Staring at light and sadness.

On our wedding day I got stuck in the elevator,
terrified because the building was round—
in every alcove the ceremony repeated.

The sense you make of me, your company
relieves me, until the thump from upstairs.
Your eyes ask me to protect you.
Maybe save your life as the mad thumper devours me.

The room is a day or spaceship floating. The work will not drop out of it, just the origin. Imagine the determination of others, puppeting you. Something will fall to fracture sleep. It's not easy to be dishonest about the system, persistent heat or its subtraction.

You've neither bone nor blood
but multitudes of brass and buried money.
Your fans will welcome you when their hands
are spent. You may bow before the mirror,
or dance for new inventions, clearer fields.
But tell us, if you know,
did honesty portend to save the world?
Did beauty?

All in favor of extremes
All for the pattern of dreams
All the bold coldness
All the wet hotness
All to forget that we bought this
All to dive with knifelike wings
All to collapse at the core when we're done
All to wake and pierce and stun
All to keep on the run
All to say that we've won
and the game, again, was all in fun

Lift up the plumes for blazing!
Hurl flames for blankets!

This is the earth without water
strung from bridges that talk.
Listen! They invite us to walk
the long side of history.

It didn't go down
like some species flaring onto the scene
or that governmental decree
that left the wetlands furrowed

if I'm an anomaly
then we're really in a glitch

we'll drop into the racket
of slums, with endless bandwidth

I gave up in favor of. I took it by force. It took you by surprise. I made a present. You decided. I bestowed. You tendered. I was taken by it. I propose a toast! We have an hour to give evidence. We'll take the water, each other, a seat, the credit. Give the wink! Give it to me! I give in, off, over, out. They take notes. We take the bribe and the letter. We take the word. Matter egresses like air from a bellows. We give rise to abandon and a bag. A bag? The bag? I take it back. I take it on, apart, and down. I take it up, over, off. I take it out. You convey. Do you take me for a fool? Take the floor. I'll take it on the chin lying down. I take exception. Take the scene to a turn, collapsing or springing. What is the take?

On that line
the reverse of you
is true

Our building floats
the world is round
edges are piles of darkness
we see the room from a floor
how leaves turning up come in as we wait

Women with candles come.
Not one makes a sound.
A priest appears closer to ghost.
It's no longer clear what matter is.

It wouldn't start on the pavement or inside an icicle or on the phone, although getting to the center of ice without melting feels the same, and the grayness, the way of removing all distinctions that concrete has is also like a mirror because you look and there is nothing truly recognizable. In the right light from the sun or street lamps, the pavement glitters and ice is something to look at, like nothing else exists or matters if it does.

All things I made sing from edges and run like dirt. The sun's the same. It burns again today.

Watch him sit. Watch him sing,
and see. A head of hair is night.
Those are alphabets, grammars,
where the river flows down.
He beats our breath to sound our mind.
The snake will rise. The pillar burn.
We will take the skulls for bowls.
Move in time. Desire. Then retire.

Call the wind a darkness:
she will not answer.
Call it gentle:
she will turn the other way.
She stretches fire to fire.
Your beard you gifted,
your pants, your thought.
Her skirt lifted leaves from trees.
Her tears soaked the world's roots.

Never come to me unclean.
I will not touch the ground.
One mistress cannot sting.
A knife, three rings, a heart.
The past is dark and sound
and smart. It's sad. It sings.
I could be a better wife—
mad, but low and light.

Waking
I saw myself a girl

a golden flame
in the golden sun
in a golden summer

a flamingo-torch
streaming toward a bicycle

Dear Zeus,

I'm little directed in epistolary matters. The instruction manual that came with the kit got stuck in a tree. I request a permanent change of address. I see through glass windows everywhere other windows. I long to touch some zephyr ruffling there.

No more do mine invite replies than grill their doubtful gestures. An assembly of propositions constitutes the enterprise. Whether in and under, or out of impossible starts, they fly, and sit beside me.

Black pigs are mine.
Their eyes of red and rage.
They say my sighs are dead,
my heart is weak.
That I've no tongue to speak.

But I will rise again,
wearing their little lies
carved inside my cheek.

1

I remember the leaves and their perception. My tongue ran from the tree when I saw the opening. Someone said the mind is a curious quilted ball.

2

No one leaves the house, crosses the street, or passes a car in a neutral state. Progress follows when the mind is busy with change.

3

The absence of light inside the country is structural. An idea of supple leaves me prone to breaking. I cannot stand idle and order nothing.

Tracing in lieu of a signature, marking an ear for ownership, or plumbing depth with knots along a sounding are odd distinctions, odd appraisals, and odd formations. Prominence is a record beside the point, so someone may be swindled. The King of Cornwall, for example, the husband of Iseult, and the uncle of her lover Tristan. Or us, because the hollow of a horse's tooth will tell its time, but moving feet suspend us.

Imagine being left here, where sound is an injured wrist or cold lung. The quick forms are strange, unlike progression. Outside of vents, we think of key fobs, the green highlight around erotica.

I do not believe nothing exists
of no consequence
no thing, not anything
in no way or degree
part or portion
no quantity to no avail
no nonentity of no substance
no nothing doing in nothing flat
for no reason
as we tunnel through something to nothing

Is the teapot moving?
I imagine sitting around.
Are there others?
Peace is outside.
Do you see planes?
Under water leaves stick.
Do you hear choppers?
I run from the window.

Restricted absolution offers other worlds, fire sweeping continents, through science, through meditation, crashing into newness when disturbance breaks. Every one's another's inertia. If the back talk balances, love leaves. And the leaves are wastebaskets or gray hair.

It's of no account
not to be buried for ages
and ferry retainers for string.

Consider your chameleonic material.
Secure the day falling.
But change too.
Dispatch suspected doubts.

No matter no proof no more
than I imagined you.
I am not so much as instant,
so much as lost
to tongue and pen and pixel
lost
where I belong and not
in thought.

Your feet are clocks. I clocked them rising and falling. You play clocks as ornaments to succeeding notes. The feet, your moving hands, and the notes are a clock. This is a clock. I'm inside listening for another clock, but the tones are unified. It's comfortable, and neatly clocked. Unclock it! Go out naked but for a pair of socks with clocks and blow it away like a clock. Say, "The data must be stable before you clock the latch."

I think I am more like a river
collecting and making intervals of noise
less shocking or branding
more like seeing polish
I want to scratch it

Waves bounce through layers and read patterns like eyes between boundaries, a kind of light-matter that fingers crust beneath crust. Direction is a stripe. It waits for polarity to reverse, plates to go flying—

I'm afraid we've slipped into a sibilant zone where even the porcelain isn't guttural. Mottled bowls clack on the table and fingers bend around plastic to produce something. Still, the pavement could be hit, jointed with creosote and glass, and layers pulsing below. Workmen peer into holes of variegated wires and read instruction manuals on city nights. Not the kind of thing you want to make a mistake on, with water spreading beneath. I suppose I'm as prepared as anyone to be electrocuted by a faucet, or drowned by a flood through a socket.

We don't notice
what is drying   or sounds banging into us
chimes through strings
but nothing through nothing
unlike light
that seems to be in the air
but waves

Black, dark-green, or blue. My letters, lightening-like, go up in flames. Up, consuming blue or gray, til all are seen and falling back—slow petals of snow coat a tiger smeared with ashes. My mind catches him, his trembling forest of desires, and rides him burning fast for nothing I can think, but what is blind.

Things move fast
and leak   for example
to validity, no more shivering

Is that logical
o asperous words   baa
stumble
            mittens
                                        not beautiful
an open mind

Not wishing to be   in a frame, I left
I leveled out
I'm sorry
            for loving subtraction, a room
                        you looking around
Your lenses are falling out
                                    Speaking
in 3rd person
because I don't want to
make pretty things
I want to stretch   sideways
          I want to pop
                    squat
                              in the cold

On the frontier
I wear a thorned envelope—
always a polymer coat.
I flex against pigs.
In near-instant evolution I mooch, intrude,
gathering inner dominion to make myself multitudes.
I conduct machineries.
It fails to baffle me.
Cloaks, this time, a button more or less.
On the border, I masquerade under surveillance
to stump my own hospitable nature
in the pandemonium of survival and death.

Summon company
to commune with the mythic city

what's to lose on a holiday
where exchange is measured by loss
and America dresses up as itself
then goes out with nothing left

but for underachieving beams in the meta-dream?
the right to bring along the dead,
to un-stick their clocks, beginning time

Thought stretches through what continues
and after a little may stand,
may be ascended. It looks better to the eye,
such as when a child perceives less,
can hear herself, and is not exhausted.

The ventures and potential perils of industry suggest a going out into, a boldness and resolution that lovers demand in more than one economy. For choosing, among so many choices, not to endeavor—perhaps to not even discover—a realm that expects no assistance from a living other is blasphemous within a religion of sacred individuals. That one must love to work for revelation drives desire—another BILLBOARD FOR IMMINENCE?

Symmetry operations, glide planes and screw axes might occur in an extended object of repeated patterns. These are the room's translations, so I keep moving. One spot elongates, another squats, but they belong to a system or relation of systems. Colors and luster are all that can be seen of the parts holding together. The walls appear to grow fast in all directions, wearing the habit of plates, but only fracturing could tell. If inside are blades and needles, the arrangement's order deceives. Either there's more than one basis and a whole network of lattices, or I'm looking at glass.

Depraved heart of the first degree,
murder *will* you out,
for such disregard like a key
opens a door of doubt.
            Forethought or not,
                        in medias res,
            don't get caught!, the justice says.
What err in likeness to you,
killing so with little rue,
but what cannot be seen
is neither dream,
                        nor true.
Call the witnesses, two,
and if not them, the city,
mop the blood,
            make it pretty!

1.

Bears see each other
breaking up space
beneath trains
fastened to a bench
dust has preferences

2.

I saw a lone girl
certainly not dancing
I was in touch with her
during all the day followed her

There would not be seeing between light, his figure, and every dark. A mirror might hold on "like a dog." He looks out, laid on top. One reflection turns, scrapes down a kind of picture. Trees are everywhere.

If I am not green and horses do not fly,
then my thymus strikes an unseen note,
and antelopes cross a sky of time.
I wear a coat of smoky petals burning red and white.
Twelve suns bounce and shape the light.
I swim the air, two, four, ten arms churning loose,
til I wear shining yellow, shining lime.
If in my hands I hold a skull, a trident, drum, and noose,
I rub the secret lining of a fire,
beat the sound of *ou*, bend down and scatter blue.

If I must unbound by words
trace a drum that drones and moans
in the hands of a blue, five-headed man,
then I'll sing through the ears of a skull,
sixteen petals around me, smoking.

Patterns of cells lighting liquid airs
strew angles of themselves
in the sum of other minds
while still systems without time
contain themselves then tip a pitcher
on the verge of pouring nothing

Daring electricity to call back,
or ironing ribbons on a state of being
is no way to invite people.
We came here for work,
not to be kept in the shadows
disagreeing on silence.

Who calls such order light,
right cracking out of night,
wheels, and reels me in his sight,
ablaze with verve and might?

I'll eat that caterpillar lust!
Cocoon and all to dust!
If gaze and gawk he must,
I'll turn his blood to rust!

Don't you like this play?
You'd prefer it rather bright, and gay —
you want fair holiday?

Come close, sit down.
Here are my wrists.
I'll hold your frown.
Give up your fists.

I have the wax.
You take the knife
and call our sister, life.

www.ingramcontent.com/pod-product-compliance
Lightning Source LLC
LaVergne TN
LVHW050943080826
845145LV00004B/1385

* 9 7 8 0 6 1 5 2 0 2 2 3 5 *